The Rock Quarry Book

The Rock Quarry Book

Michael Kehoe

Carolrhoda Books, Inc., Minneapolis

The author and publisher would like to thank Cy Zierden, President, Delano Granite, Inc., Delano, Minnesota, for his assistance in the preparation of this book.

LIBRARY OF CONGRESS CATALOGING IN PUBLICATION DATA

Kehoe, Michael.
    The rock quarry book.

    SUMMARY: A step-by-step description of preparing rock for building from digging it out of the ground to the final polishing.

    1. Quarries and quarrying—Juvenile literature. 2. Building stones—Juvenile literature. [1. Quarries and quarrying. 2. Building stones] I. Title.

TN277.K35   622'.36   980-28165
ISBN 0-87614-142-4

1   2   3   4   5   6   7   8   9   10   87   86   85   84   83   82   81

A Note from the Author

I cannot remember a time when I haven't been fascinated with the land. I grew up in Duluth, Minnesota—an area with a wonderfully diverse landscape that ranges from high hills to deep valleys, from small streams to the ocean-like expanse of Lake Superior. Much of my childhood was spent exploring the hills and beaches, making imaginary conquests and claiming territories, or pretending I stood on the deck of a freighter or sailed in a balloon overlooking it all.

One of the places that most captured my imagination, but was strictly forbidden to me, was the gravel quarry. The quarry buzzed and roared with the sounds of cranes and trains and trucks. But the scene of all this activity was securely fenced in, and workers watched the gates to keep curious children away from the dangers within.

So I watched from the hills. From a favorite spot with my back against a rock I would sit for hours and see the land transformed. The trees were removed first, then the boulders, and finally the grass, as easily, it seemed, as one removes the glasses, plates, and tablecloth from a table. Their foundation, like a table, lay revealed.

To those of you who, like me, are filled with wonder at what lies beneath the earth we see, I dedicate this book, and also . . .

. . . to my nephew Johnny

What does this rock quarry . . .

. . . have in common with this building?

The rock that is taken out of the quarry . . .

. . . is cut and shaped to become the stone surface of the building.

The rock must go through many stages before it can be used for the surface of a building, for a sidewalk, or for statues and monuments.

Shipping

Hoisting

Cutting

The Quarry

Use

Artwork

Polishing

Sizing

The first stage takes place at the quarry.

The Quarry

A quarry is a place where rock is removed from the ground. This is a granite quarry. All of the rock taken out of this pit is of one type—granite.

A quarry begins as a small hole . . .

. . . that is ten feet deep.

As more and more rock is removed, the hole becomes deeper and deeper.

Years later the quarry will be very deep, like this one. Work on this pit was begun in 1974. Since each level is ten feet deep, the workers at the bottom of the pit are 90 feet from the surface.

Cutting

These men are working at the bottom of the granite pit. They use a large drill to cut the rock into blocks that can be lifted out of the pit. The drill they are using is powered by compressed air.

The drill bit has four teeth to chisel through the rock.

The air flows through a hose to the drill where it causes the drill bit to spin.

All these lines are drill holes.

Instead of a drill, this man is using a jet torch to cut the rock. The flame is so hot and powerful that it burns a path through the granite.

The path the torch cuts is clean and smooth, unlike the rough, jagged path the drill makes. Both the torch and the drill make a lot of noise and blow dirt and smoke all over. Workers must protect their ears when they are using these tools.

But whether the rock is cut with a drill or a jet torch, the cut is always ten feet deep.

Hoisting

Huge derricks sit on the rim of the pit ready to hoist the cut blocks of granite to the top.

Each derrick turns on its base so its boom can be swung to the right location.

A derrick operator sits in the power house high atop the machinery, waiting for a signal to begin lifting. At the bottom of the pit, chains are fastened to a block with hooks that fit into holes drilled into the granite.

When the chains are secure, a signal is given to begin lifting. Another worker at the top of the pit passes the signal to the derrick operator.

Now the operator goes into action. He pulls the levers and pushes the buttons that operate the derrick. The gears begin to turn. The winch strains as it begins to wind up the cable hooked to the block.

Slowly and carefully the block is lifted up and out of the pit, where it will be stacked with other blocks waiting to be shipped to the mill.

When the granite block has been safely removed, a front-end loader is lowered to the bottom of the pit to clean up.

Then it's time for a break.

Shipping

When enough blocks have been cut, they are loaded onto a railroad flatcar and shipped to the mill.

A crane is used to lift the blocks onto the flatcar. Each is carefully placed to make certain it won't slip off during shipment. Records are kept of every block shipped out.

Sizing

At the mill, the granite blocks are made into many useful products. First though, they must be cut into smaller sizes.

The blocks are cut into slabs by tightly stretched, steel wires. It takes eight hours to cut through one block.

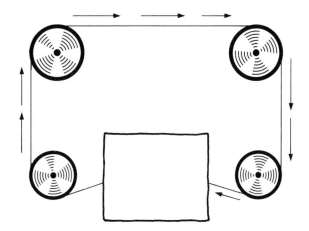

Then the slabs are moved to another area where they are cut even smaller with a circular saw. The saw has a steel blade that spins like a wheel. It cuts very fast.

Polishing

The dull surfaces of the granite slabs are now polished until they shine like tabletops.

Polishing is done by a huge machine which holds a polishing disk that spins as it moves back and forth over the slab.

The disk holds felt pads which rub on the granite and slowly make it smooth. The pads are very soft.

Artwork

Sometimes customers want designs carved into the surface of the stone.

Drawing requires a steady hand.

An artist, working at a special table, first draws the design and lettering on paper.

After it has been drawn, the design is transferred onto the stone.

Later the design will be cut.

The Quarry Cutting Hoisting Shipping Sizing Polishing Artwork Use
Use

At last the stone is ready to use. It might be used for a park memorial like this one, which was made right at the mill.

It might be used for a floor. This granite floor will last many years.

This church was made entirely of stone. After many years the weather has loosened some of the stones, so workers must climb up and repair them.

The dark stone on this building has a very beautiful natural design in it. The stone was polished to a high gloss to make the design stand out so we can see it clearly.

The End